*There's a sucker born every minute … and a con man every three.*

— P.T. Barnum

*You may not be able to fool all the people all the time, but you might as well give it your best shot.*

— Anonymous

*If we don't change direction soon, we'll end up where we're going.*

— Prof. Irwin Corey

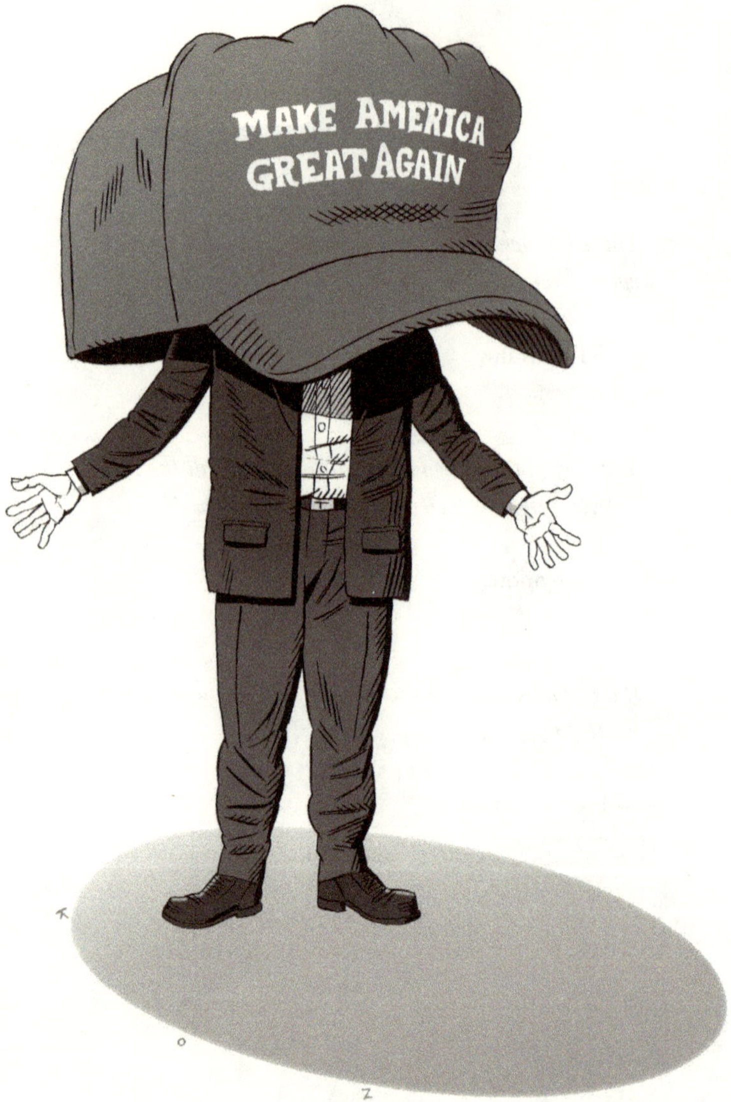
MAKE AMERICA
GREAT AGAIN

# TALK
## TO THE
# HAIR

A Look Back
at the First
100 Days of
the Trump
Presidency

by L.K. Peterson

Illustrated by
Martin Kozlowski

Cover Art by Deborah Berk
Back Cover Art by Martin Kozlowski

Material from this book first appeared with the same title in eBook form and on the website antfarmersalmanac.com



For more on Now What Media Books,
please visit nowwhatmedia.com/nowwhatbooks.html

Check out these other
Now What Books
at nowwhatmedia.com

**Flick and Flak:**
**More Poison Capsule Reviews**

**The Golem's Voice**

**Further Adventures:**
**Now What Anthology No. 1**

**PK in the Terrarium**

**Downtown Drowned**

**The Da Vinci Cold**

**Go the F\*\*k Back to Work!**

**Fairly Grim Tales**

**Love the Sinner**
**Hate the Cinema**

**Gertrude's Follies**

**INX Battle Lines**

**2012 Doomsday Planner**

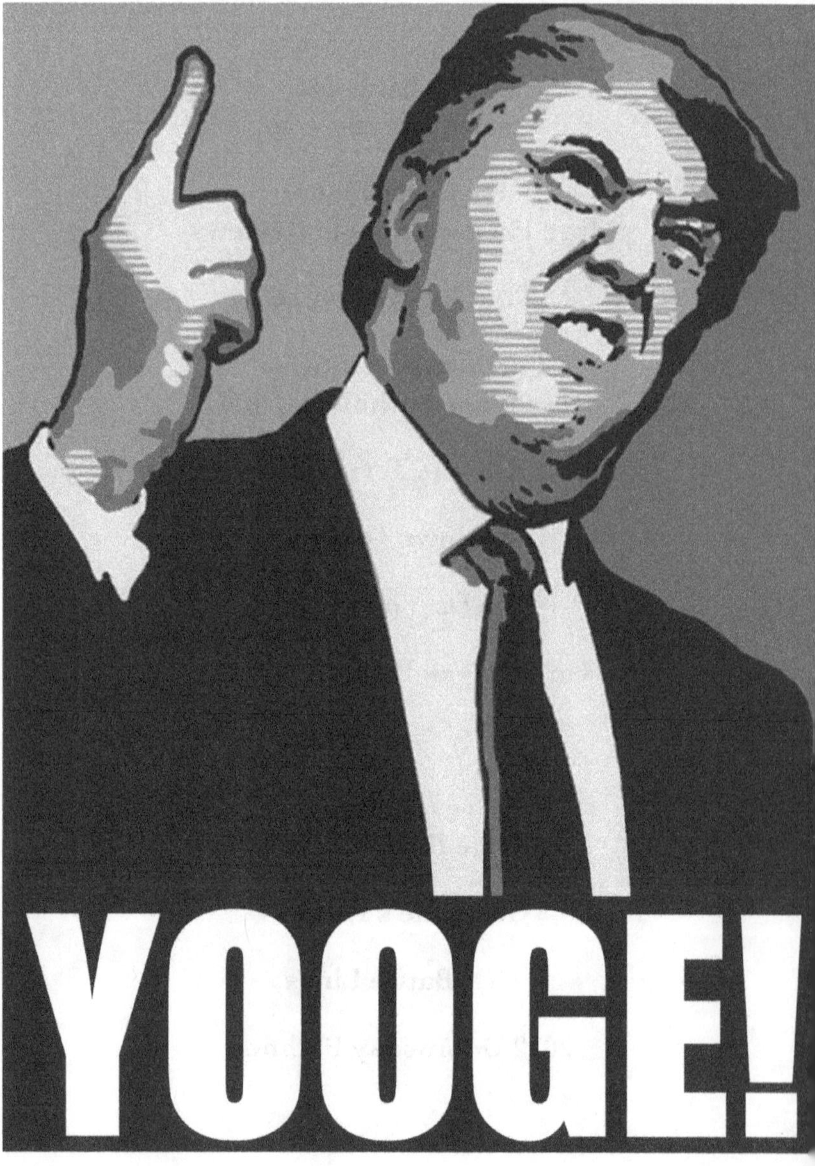
YOOGE!

# INTRODUCTION

Swept into office by a coalition of supporters angry at the political process and everyone in it, Donald J. Trump defied experts' expectations, pundits' predictions, conventional wisdom and common sense. The reality TV star and real estate-mogul's brash unfiltered style, oversize personality and vow to "Make America totally classy again" drew large and enthusiastic crowds throughout the campaign, ultimately winning "The Donald" the presidency over candidates once thought to be as unbeatable as they were inevitable. As a victorious Trump crowed triumphantly on election night, "We are going to be *huge*! We will be the envy of all the losers who aren't us."

In the weeks before the inauguration, president-elect Trump and vice president-elect Kardashian began vetting potential cabinet secretaries in a series of televised "Celebrity Apprentice" style competitions. How many of these contestant-nominees would ultimately be confirmed by Congress was anybody's

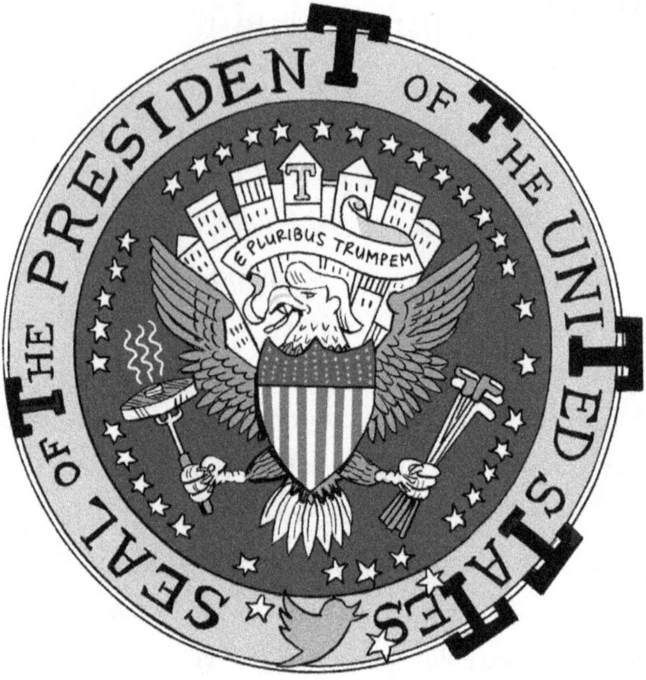
SEAL OF THE PRESIDENT OF THE UNITED STATES
E PLURIBUS TRUMPEM
T

guess although most of the commentariat agreed Howie Mandel was a lock for Secretary of Agriculture.

After taking the oath of office on the same Bible used to swear-in Ronald Reagan (only when told he couldn't use a copy of "The Art of the Deal"), Trump gazed out over the sea of "Trump 2016" campaign caps, tri-corn and tinfoil hats stretching the length of the National Mall. Now the 45th president of the United States of America, Mr. Trump found himself briefly overcome by an unfamiliar sensation (aides would later identify it as humility).

In his inaugural address to the nation, the new president reiterated his campaign theme, "Speak Loudly and Stick it to Everybody." Peppered with boiler plate stump speech barbs at the political and media elite, his remarks included newly minted scorn for vanquished opponents — "Crooked Hillary" became "Cooked Hillary"— and vows of retribution against all who had spoken out against him, "I will tell you this about President Trump, I don't ever forget and I don't often forgive."

A few crowd-pleasing zingers later, Trump addressed his administration's philosophy and policy goals. "Some people say government isn't about making money," he shouted to the adoring throng, "Those people are losers. Anything that can be done can be done for a profit! It's what America does best; it's what we do, period! Good times or bad, somebody — usually me — makes a buck. Prosperity is the best kind of patriotism, and the only kind that counts!"

In conclusion, President Trump promised to "Take us back to the glory of the past and make that glorious past our future again," vowing to "Restore the financial might of this great nation to the halcyon days of the '80s... the 1880s when the country was run by and for men like me who made vast fortunes and kept those fortunes because Washington didn't tell them what they could and couldn't do or how they could and couldn't do it. That's how America's gonna work again now that I'm in charge!"

With those words and to thunderous applause, the Trump Era began. What follows is a day-by-day account of its first 100 days.

— L.K. Peterson, May 1, 2017

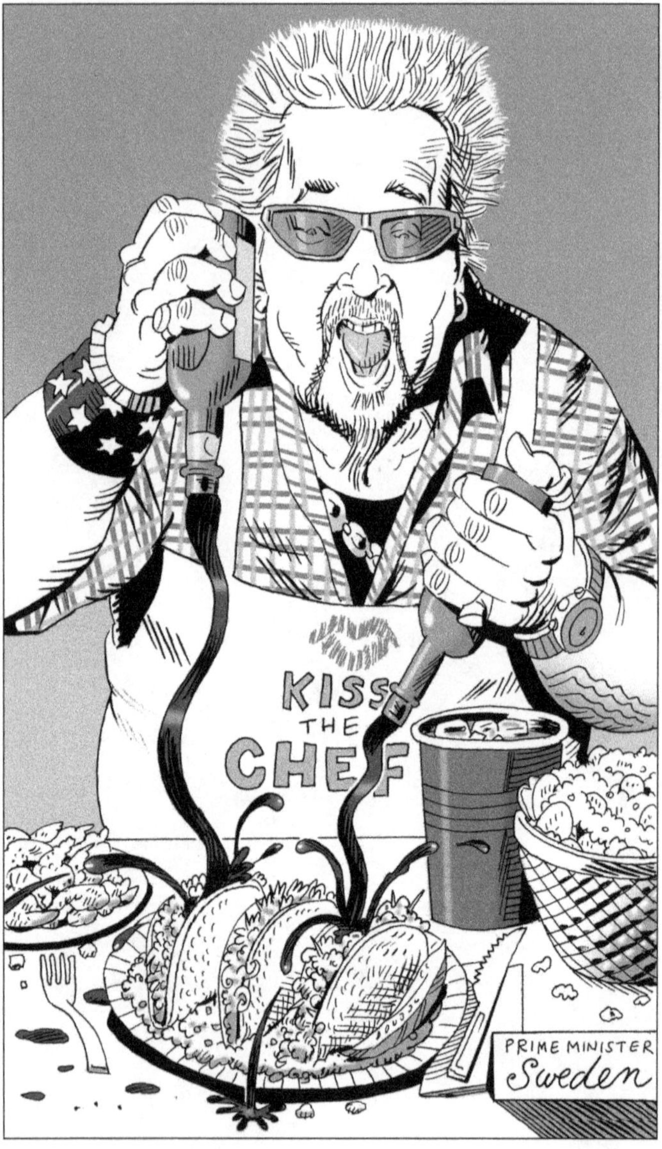
KISS THE CHEF
PRIME MINISTER
Sweden

## Day 1

Thousands of Inaugural Ball revelers are injured attempting "The Combover," a dance based on the bending, folding, swooping and twisting motions believed necessary to get the president's hair into place.

## Day 2

Rachel Maddow, Jon Stewart, Ivana Trump and Marla Maples are deported.

## Day 3

Guy Fieri is appointed White House chef. He will serve a single one-year term after which he will be succeeded by the winner of a televised competition cooking show.

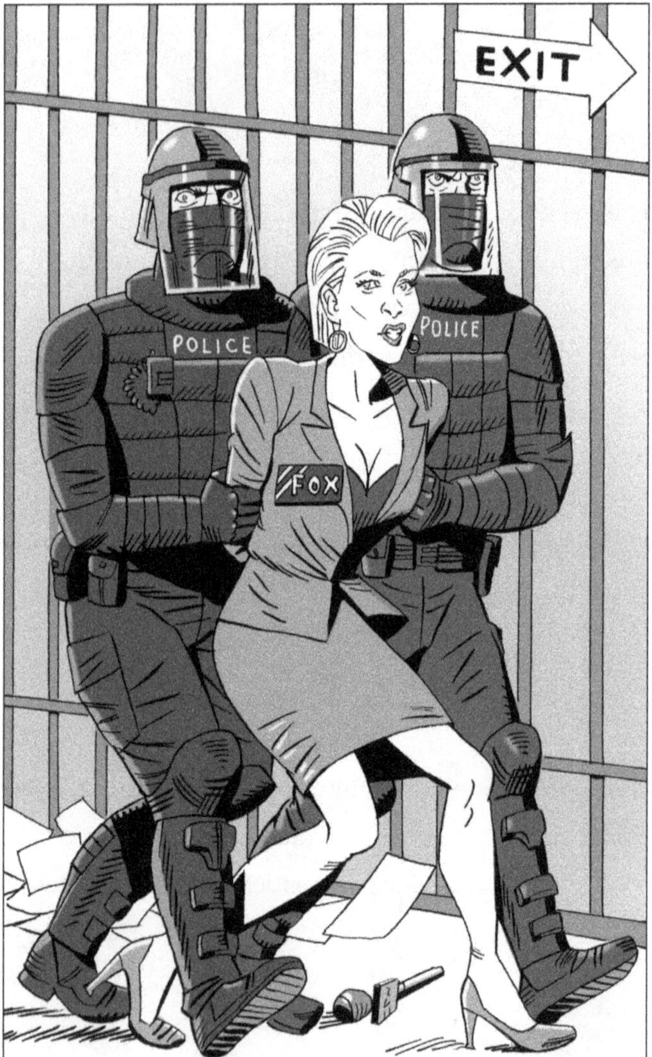
EXIT
POLICE
POLICE
FOX

## Day 4

Despite having proper press credentials, Megyn Kelly is denied access to the White House briefing room.

## Day 5

Psychologists diagnose a widespread new condition, "The DT's," described as that moment of shock upon waking from a deep sleep and remembering Donald Trump is actually president of the United States.

## Day 6

The president announces "Operation Return to Sender," a program under which suspected undocumented immigrants from Mexico, "Or wherever," are deported and their jobs given to unemployed American citizens. "Sure," acknowledges Trump, "These are mostly loser jobs but hey, losers can't be choosers and now at least you've got a job. You're welcome."

## Day 7

Because of her long experience living within sight of it, Sarah Palin is appointed ambassador to Russia; the press corps dubs her, "Our Moron in Moscow."

## Day 8

By Executive Order, pizza must now be eaten with a knife and fork.

## Day 9

Air Force One is retired and all executive branch transportation is contracted out to the newly revived Trump Air. Questioned about the legality and propriety of Trump Air's exclusive no-bid government contract, Secretary of Transportation Chris Christie assures reporters, "Absolutely 100% no wrongdoing will be found by the independent investigation I will personally conduct right after lunch."

## Day 10

Using the power of presidential appointments to punish as well as reward, Trump forcibly makes Hillary Clinton the United States' Ambassador to Antarctica, air dropping her onto the South Pole in the dead of night.

## Day 11

Camp David is renamed "Camp Donald."

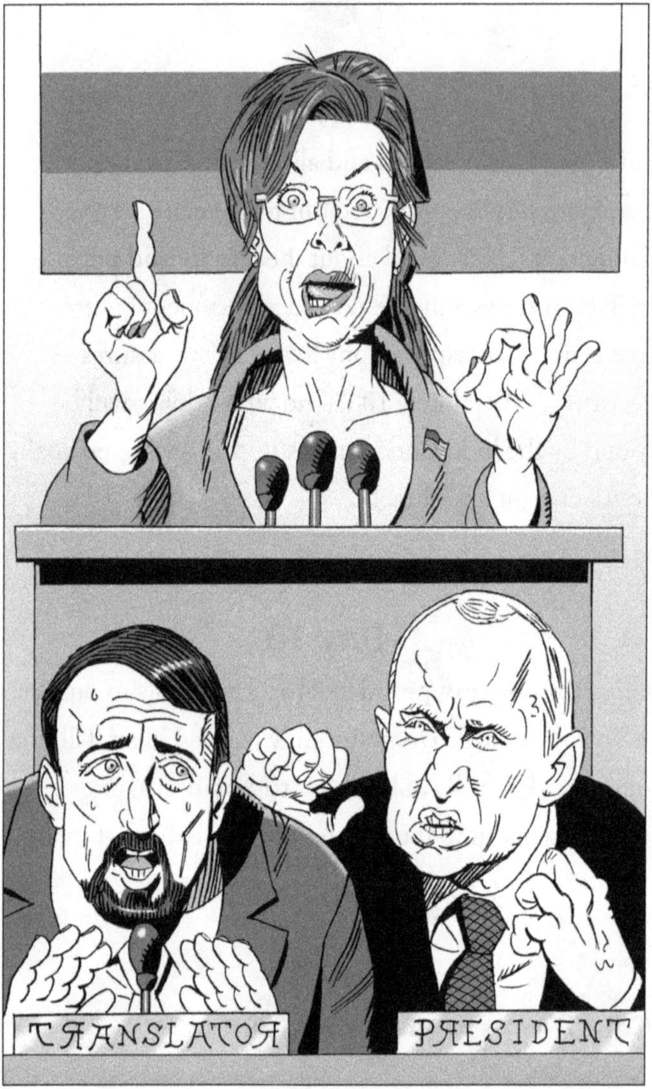
TRANSLATOR
PRESIDENT

## Day 12

In the days before groundbreaking of the fence between the U.S. and Mexico, several hundred Mexican nationals sneak across the border disguised as construction workers. While many stay around and help build the wall as day laborers, most claim they are contractors who will "Be back next Tuesday" and are never seen again.

## Day 13

Ambassador Palin's Russian translator is fired when he tells Vladimir Putin, "I don't know what she's trying to say or even what she thinks she means." When a second translator is brought in and faithfully repeats everything Palin says in Russian, word for word, syntax and all, he is fired for being drunk on the job.

## Day 14

After Mexico refuses to pay for the wall along its border with the U.S., construction costs have to be offset by donors who, in exchange for their money, get a plaque bearing their name placed on the fence; the higher the contribution, the more prominent the plaque.

## Day 15

Furious at the Mexican government and frustrated by the legal and bureaucratic tangles delaying implementation of his anti-immigrant and anti-Muslim policies, President Trump creates the "Illegal Alienation Act" and proclaims through Executive Order that anyone "suspiciously foreign-looking" will be deported to Mexico where they can sort them out.

## Day 16

Border Fence construction begins. Two teams composed of private contractors supplemented by units of the Army Corps of Engineers start in San Diego, California and Brownsville, Texas, respectively, and race to meet in the middle.

## Day 17

First presidential haircut takes place on the tarmac as Trump boards "Marine One," his hair flies straight up on end and a chunk of it gets sliced off by the helicopter's rotor blades.

BEST PREZ EVER

## Day 18

The White House Gift Shop adds a section devoted exclusively to Trump brand merchandise, including Trump cologne, ties, mineral water, real estate listings, all of his books, and a rack of "collector-quality" New Jersey Generals memorabilia. "The Donald" dashboard bobble heads are especially big sellers.

## Day 19

To the surprise of many, Trump accelerates the normalizing of relations with Cuba, offering fast-tracked U.S. territorial status and even hinting at eventual statehood.

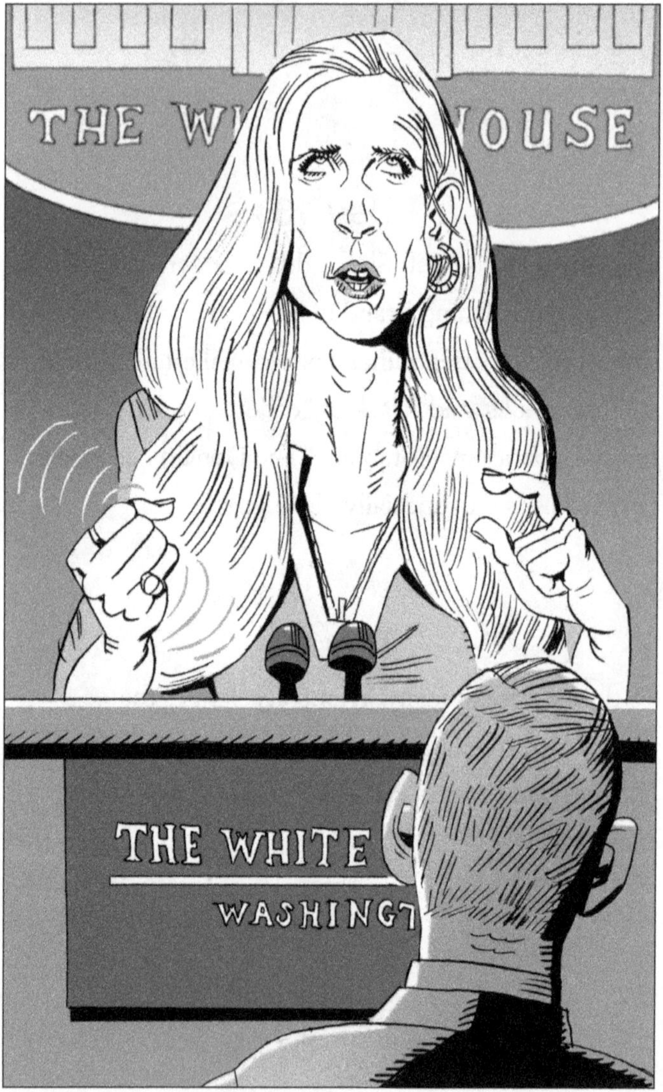
THE W
OUSE
THE WHITE
WASHING

## Day 20

White House Press Secretary Ann Coulter quits after three weeks on the job, irked at reporters' insistence that her responses to questions be more than just eye rolling and swipes at their masculinity. The president's first choice as Coulter's replacement, Geraldo Rivera, is unavailable, having been caught up in an INS sweep ("He looked kinda Mexican" said the arresting officer) and is currently detained somewhere in the Yucatan..

## Day 21

At the press event introducing his now-confirmed cabinet, President Trump refers to them as, "Your new Board of Directors."

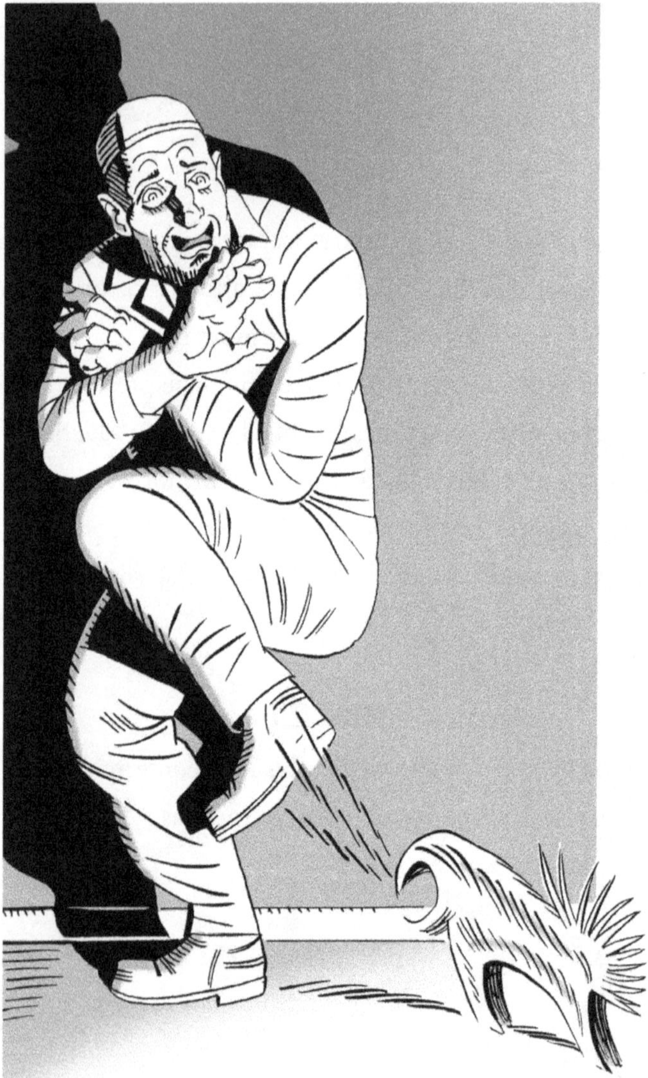

## Day 22

The president's hair is declared "First Pet" by a snarky political gossip website. After an Internet contest for naming it, "Trumpet" is declared the winner.

## Day 23

Trump Steaks are designated the "Official Meat of America."

## Day 24

The White House is officially renamed the Trump White House®. Additionally, any Trump property bearing his name is designated a "Weekend Trump White House®" and, as such, a totally legitimate tax write-off.

## Day 25

The Immigration and Naturalization Service is militarized.

## Day 26

On his first official trip to that nation, Marco Rubio, Trump's "Ambassador and Presumptive Cuban Territorial Governor" is taken aback by the hostile response to his arrival, when he is pelted with rotten fruit and vintage car parts.

## Day 27

President Trump "fixes" Obamacare by outlawing use of the word "Obamacare." Runner-up GOP candidates all acknowledge that this was pretty much their plan too.

## Day 28

As work on the Border Fence progresses 24/7, projected costs skyrocket far beyond the original budget. Private donations fall short, so corporate sponsorship and naming rights for mile-long stretches are offered. A high-stakes bidding war surpasses expectations and, with the flood of new funding, construction surges ahead of schedule.

## Day 29

Upon learning their code names for him are "Hairbag One" and "POUTUS," President Trump dismisses his entire Secret Service detail, replacing them with several large guys from Atlantic City, all of whom answer to the name, "Vinny."

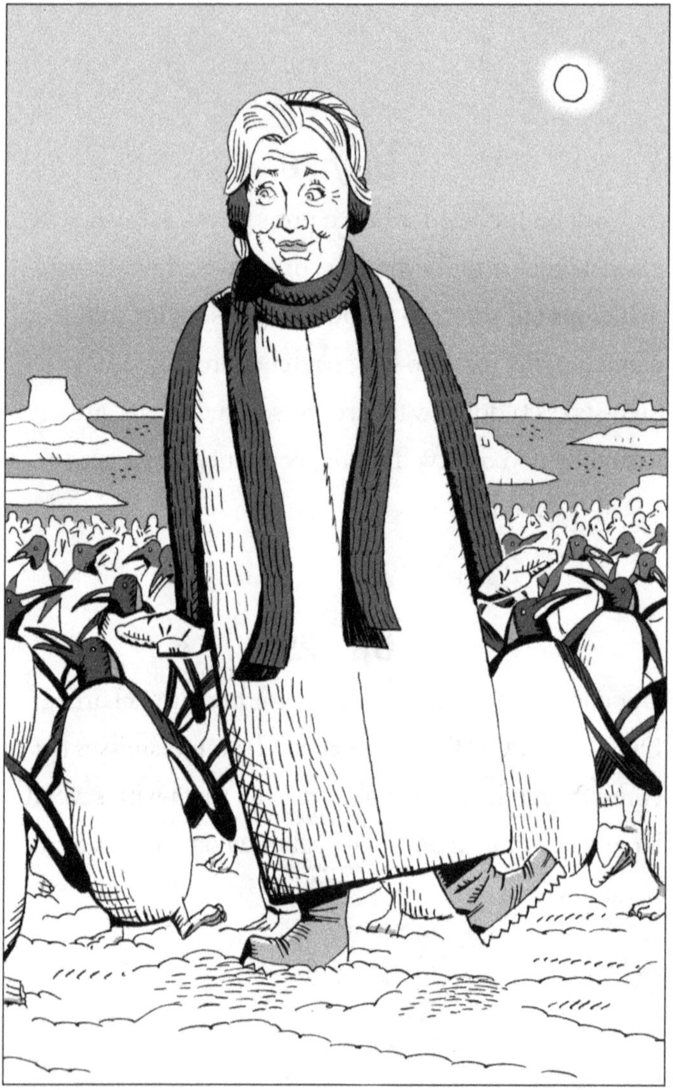

## Day 30

Relief that the reported $13.7 billion price tag for the Inaugural Balls was a typographical error is short-lived when the actual number turns out to be $17.3 billion.

## Day 31

Aides explain to a disappointed Trump that, even though he is president of the USA, he doesn't get to host, judge or attend the Miss USA Pageant.

## Day 32

Scientific researchers at a remote base in Antarctica report the meteoric rise to power of a "very alpha female" among the penguins. Despite her low approval ratings and not actually being a penguin herself, her hard-line position on sea lion and killer-whale violence, promise to put two fish in every nest, and vow to close the Volcker Rule's hedge fund loophole win her widespread support.

## Day 33

On a "Very Special Episode" of the ancestry TV show, "Who Do You Think You Are?" DNA test results "reveal" that Trump is descended from every native-American tribe that ever existed. He declares all his properties are now "reservations" and eligible for the development of casinos.

## Day 34

Card-counting is made a federal crime.

## Day 35

The Trump administration's negotiating stance toward Iran — "How about you give us all your oil then go fuck yourselves and maybe we don't bomb you back to the stone age" — proves as controversial as it is ineffective.

## Day 36

President The Donald acknowledges he carries a concealed handgun on his person at all times; oddsmakers have it at 20-to-one that it's concealed someplace in his hair.

## Day 37

By Executive Order, instead of money for tax refunds, the IRS will issue tax-payers gaming chips equal in value to their amount due, redeemable at any Trump-owned casino resort in the continental U.S.

## Day 38

Rumors that the highly reflective gold tiles being applied to the White House® exterior are solar panels turn out to be untrue.

## Day 39

The President announces his Zero-Tolerance policy for any undocumented Mexicans in the U.S., "I don't care how long you've been here or whether you're old or new."

## Day 40

New Mexico renames itself "East Arizona" just to be on the safe side.

## Day 41

Chipotle is put on an INS watch list.

# Day 42

"Outrage Fatigue" is the only explanation for the nearly total lack of response when the Trump campaign's list of supporters' names and email addresses (known to insiders as "The Dipshits Who Drank the Sucker Punch") is offered for sale on eBay. Deemed "priceless" by advertisers and marketers who see in it a mother lode of reliably gullible consumers, the winning bidder — at $122 million — is a "Nigerian Prince."

# Day 43

In New York City for the first time since taking office, Trump breaks with the tradition of staying in the Presidential Suite of the Waldorf Astoria Hotel, saying, "That dump? I've got classier rooms in my garage!"

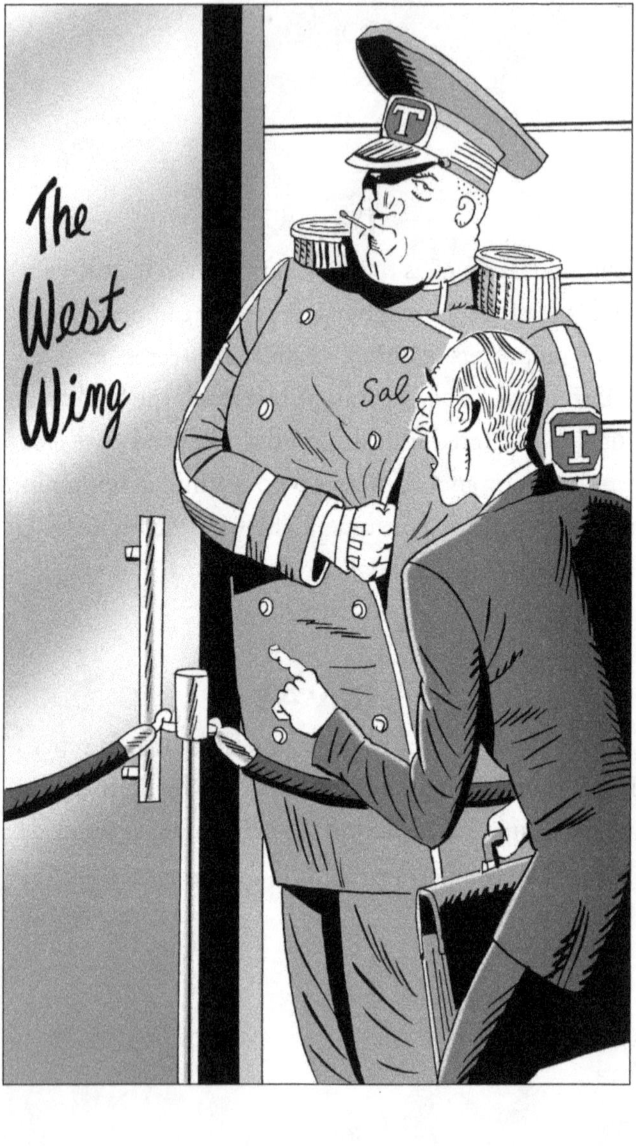
The West Wing
Sal
T
T

## Day 44

The Oval Office is redecorated as a trophy room packed with the mounted heads, horns, hooves and hides of various animals—many endangered—bagged on safari by presidential offspring. The polar bear rug at the center of the room, however, is from Hugh Hefner's private collection, picked up at a Playboy Mansion yard sale.

## Day 45

All of the Marine Honor guard at the Trump White House® resign rather than wear the Park Avenue doorman-style uniforms the president has had designed for them.

## Day 46

The Trump White House® honor guard is replaced by several large guys from Atlantic City who answer to "Sal," and who don't seem to mind the knee-length maroon overcoats with gold-fringed epaulettes."

## Day 47

Appearing before a general assembly of the United Nations, the president outlines "The Donald Doctrine" in which all U.S. foreign aid will be renegotiated into terms more advantageous to the U.S., i.e., "You want some quid? First, show me the quo!"

## Day 48

After Trump's foreign policies are denounced on the floor of the United Nations, delegates residing in Trump-owned apartment buildings suddenly find themselves without hot water.

## Day 49

Ignoring increasingly frantic requests from the besieged U.S. diplomatic mission in Havana and the tearful pleas of the man's family in Florida, Trump steadfastly refuses to recall Marco Rubio from Cuba.

## Day 50

An informal weekly press conference at which the president's more outlandish, extra-constitutional and possibly illegal remarks are "explained" and "given context" is dubbed "The Walk-A-Back."

## Day 51

It is noticed that Trump remains indoors all day whenever the National Weather Service issues a "Strong Wind Advisory" for the DC Metro area. Rumors circulate start that he's doing so to avoid risking a "Bad Hair Day" which quickly becomes the go-to euphemism for any presidential setback or blunder.

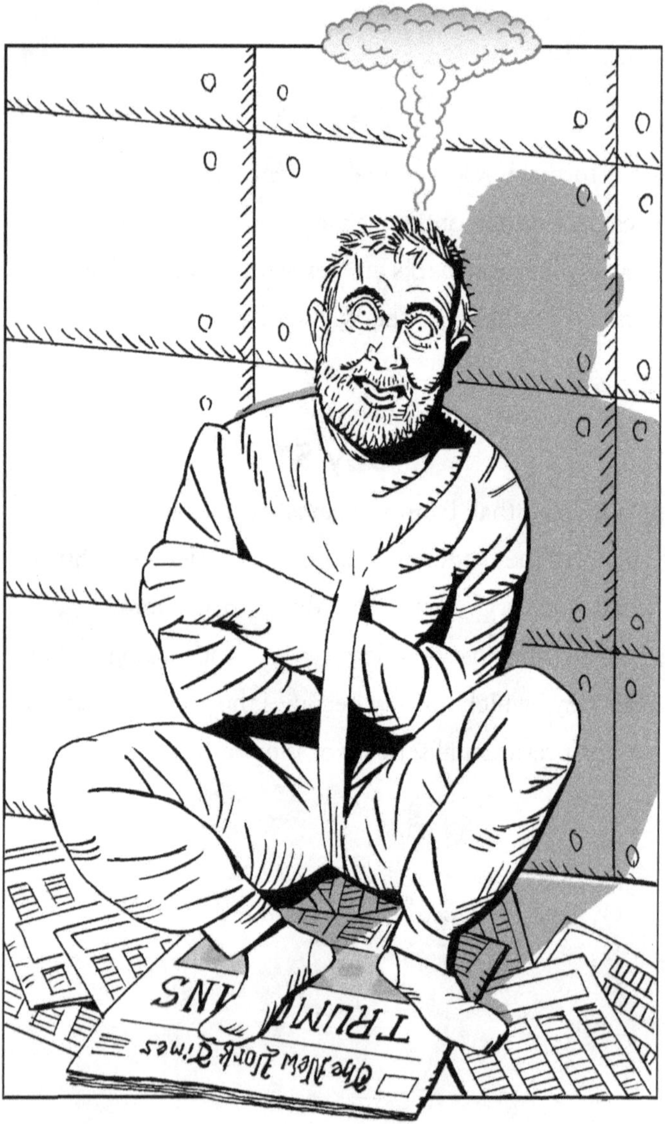
The New York Times

# Day 52

After he writes a series of columns: "This Can't Really Be Happening, Can It?", "Has Everyone Lost Their Minds?!", "Will Somebody Impeach This Jerk Before He Destroys the Country?!?", "I Don't Even Know Why I Bother Anymore." and "Well, I Guess This is How It's Gonna Be, Then…", the New York Times announces Paul Krugman's sabbatical to a nice, quiet Greek island without television, radio, wifi, or contact with the outside world.

# Day 53

Recipients of a zinger from President Trump are said to have been "T-Boned."

# Day 54

White House sources report the president is furious when informed he can't nominate Judge Judy, Judge Joe Brown or Simon Cowell to the Supreme Court and is threatening a recess appointment of Gary Busey.

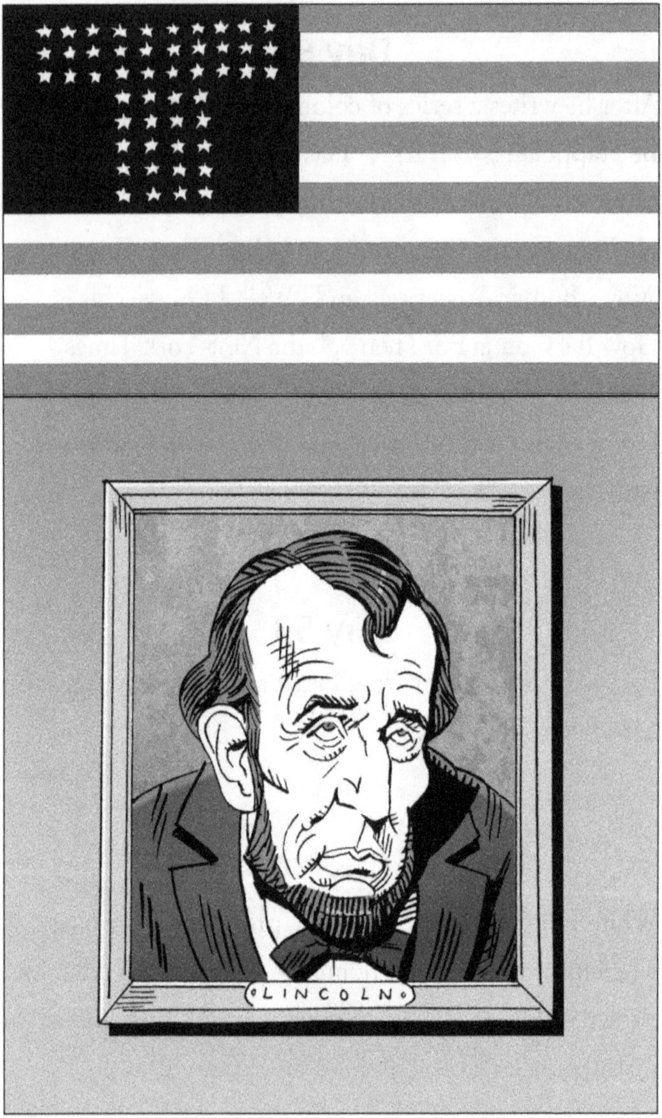
LINCOLN

## Day 55

Plans for a redesigned American flag with the stars arranged as a capital "T" are scuttled after swift and negative public reaction. A handful of the prototypes are said to hang in the Lincoln Bedroom, at Camp Donald and in the Presidential Suites of several Trump-owned casino resorts.

## Day 56

In the wake of corporate sponsors vying for naming rights of sections of the border fence the question becomes what to call the thing in its entirety. Various catchy nicknames are tested ("Burrito Wall," "Cactus Curtain," "The Trump Line," "The Great Wall of Shiny"), but it is ultimately decided that "Border Fence" pretty much says it all.

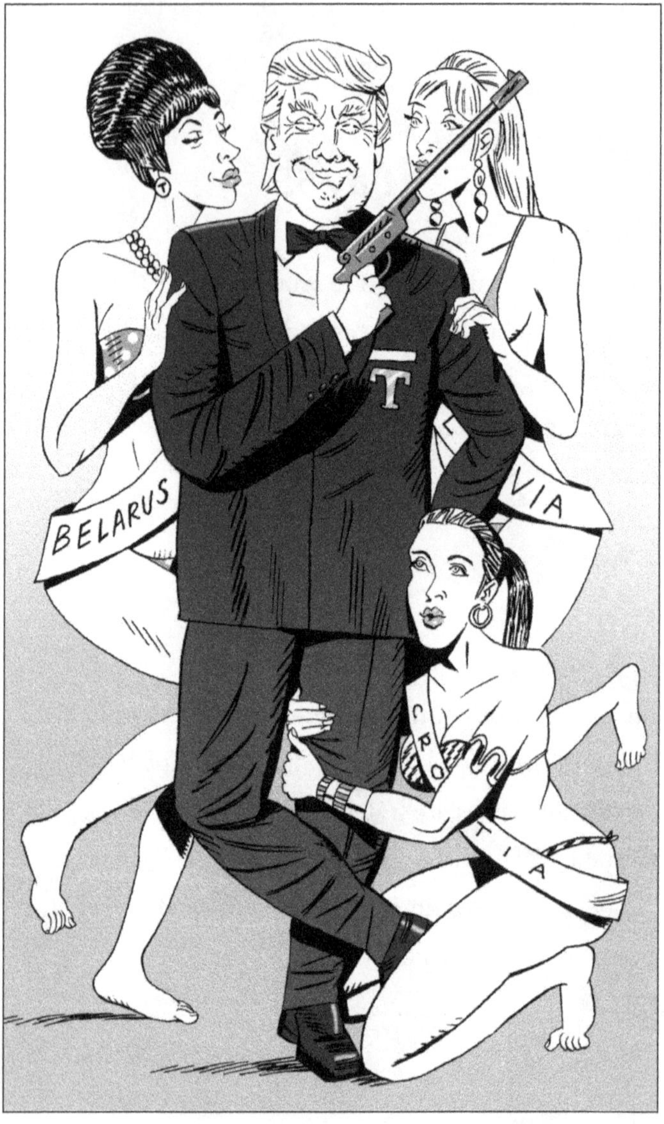
BELARUS
VIA
CRO
TIA

## Day 57

Sports Illustrated announces that its next Swimsuit Issue photo shoot will take place at Mar-A-Lago, Trump's Florida Trump White House® and that the president will appear in many of the spreads "Fully clothed, mind you," according to the magazine's editors.

## Day 58

The U.S. military is privatized and the Pentagon leased to the Halliburton Corporation. Trump notes admiringly that, "Halliburton has totally got what it takes to start a war, keep it going, and make a buck in the process!"

## Day 59

As part of his proposed overhaul of Social Security, in lieu of benefits, payments, Trump offers recipients gaming chips equal in value to their benefit amount, redeemable at any Trump-owned casino resort in the continental U.S.

## Day 60

The presidential anthem "Hail to the Chief" is replaced with Sinatra's "My Way."

## Day 61

First Chef Fieri complains about the Mexicans in his Trump White House® kitchen being rounded up and deported, saying, "I can't run this place without people who know what they're doing… it's not like this is Congress or something!"

## Day 62

Fieri is fired as Trump White House® chef, allegedly for signing a deal to publish a tell-all cookbook entitled "The Art of the Meal: Dishing on the Donald's Dinner."

## Day 63

After an escalation of clashes in Havana between residents and the growing number of returning exiles, communication with ambassador Rubio is lost.

## Day 64

Printing of U.S. currency is outsourced to China ("Most of our money belongs to them, anyway, they can just print up however much we owe them").

## Day 65

Hours after a televised interview in which former Senator John McCain scathingly criticizes Trump, his administration and everyone who voted it in, the Veterans Administration suspends benefits to anyone who was captured.

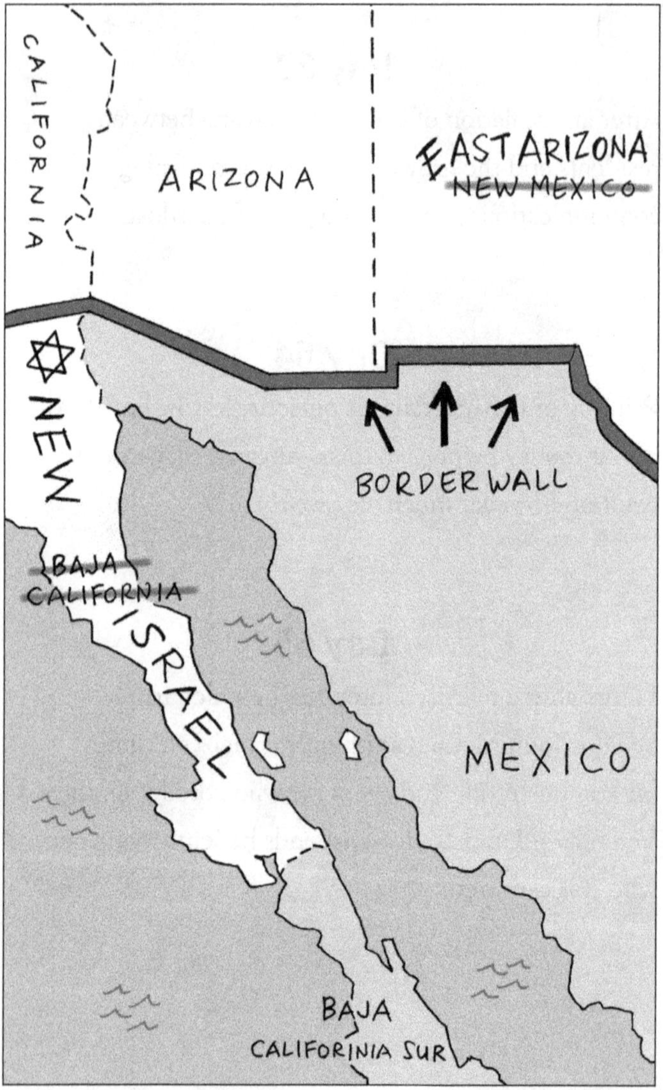
CALIFORNIA
ARIZONA
EAST ARIZONA
NEW MEXICO
NEW
ISRAEL
BAJA
CALIFORNIA
BORDER WALL
MEXICO
BAJA
CALIFORINIA SUR

## Day 66

Despite his words in support of Israel during the campaign ("Many on my accounting staff are Jewish, and I myself enjoy the occasional bagel."), American Jews are deeply unnerved when President Trump's secret plan for peace in the Middle East turns out to be the relocation of Israel to Baja California ("Better weather, beaches on both sides, no Arabs!").

## Day 67

Hawaii announces its intent to secede from the U.S. on condition that former president Obama accept the position of "Big Kahuna-for-Life."

## Day 68

The Border Fence is completed near El Paso, Texas.

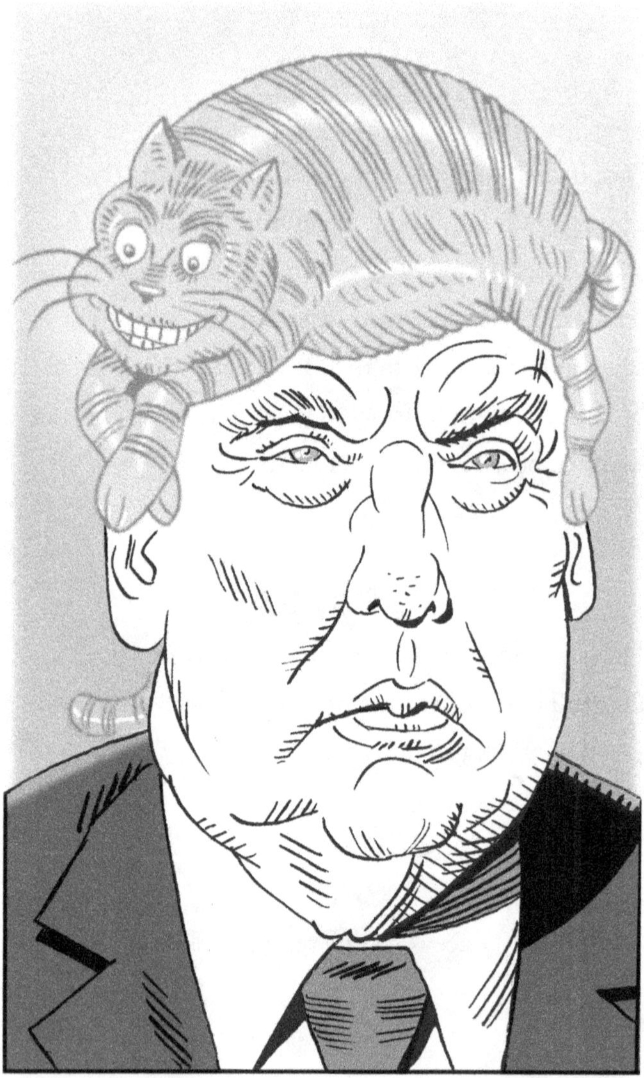

## Day 69

A puppet character of Trumpet (a modified Garfield the Cat plush toy), who speaks belligerent nonsense in the president's voice, becomes a regular comedy routine entitled, "Talk to the Hair" on the Conan O'Brien Show.

## Day 70

President Trump "christens" the Border Fence by hammering at an oversize gold-plated nail on the final panel. The irony that Taco Bell is the corporate sponsor of this particular section is lost on no one.

## Day 71

There is consternation that the "Beautiful Door" in the Border Fence President Trump promised turns out to be not some metaphor for a path to citizenship but a heavily guarded drawbridge over a piranha-filled moat nicknamed "Checkpoint Donald."

## Day 72

INS units stationed along the border for "Detainee Deportation Duty" (also known as "Operation Good Riddance") are issued catapults along with conventional ordinance.

## Day 73

The Walk-A-Back event is extended to Mondays, Wednesdays and Fridays.

## Day 74

Canadian Premier Justin Trudeau proposes an electrified chain-link fence separating the U.S. from his country to stem the tide of U.S. refugees fleeing north.

## Day 75

Displeased that Congress is dragging its feet on so may
of his policy proposals, Trump "fires" them. Many
newer members, elected on his coattails, pack up their
offices and head for home before being informed he
can't actually do that.

## Day 76

Told a president doesn't have the authority to "fire"
Congress, Trump responds ominously, "We'll see about
that."

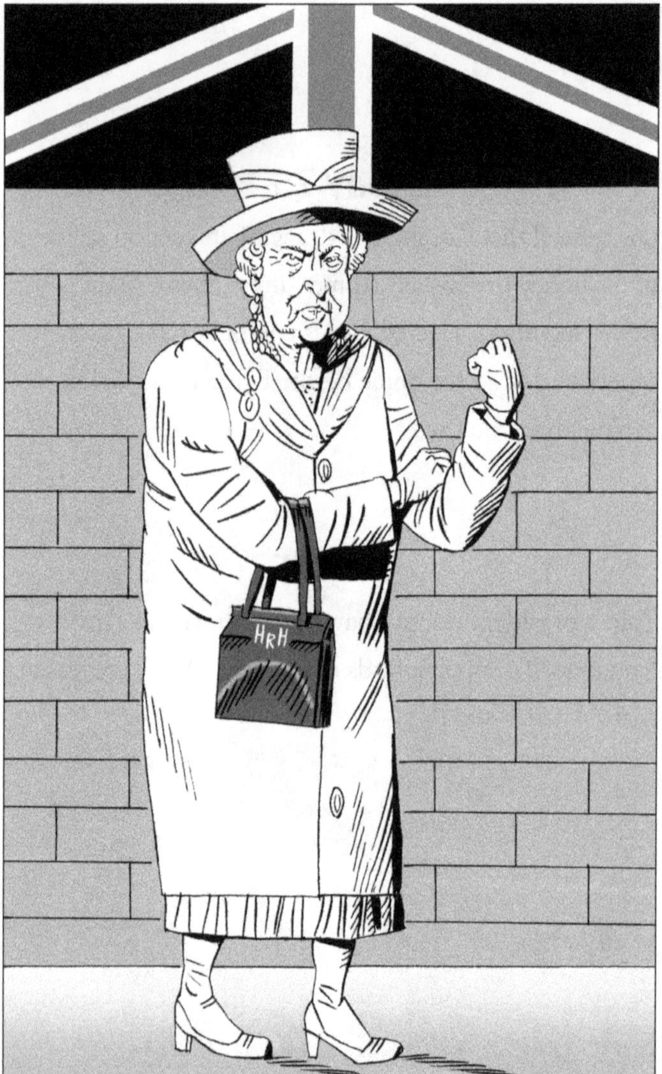
HRH

# Day 77

President Trump is declared persona-non-grata in Germany after making rude (even for him) remarks about Chancellor Andrea Merkel's attractiveness, fitness to lead, sexual orientation, IQ, and personal hygiene.

# Day 78

In a rare display of international unity, every nation with a female head of state—including Antarctica's newly crowned "Empress of All Penguins"—announces that President Trump is "Not welcome on our sovereign soil." Queen Elizabeth II of Great Britain speaks for the entire group, stating, "We are not amused."

## Day 79

Residents along both the Mexico and U.S. sides of the Border Fence complain about the light coming from the advertising signs atop it at all hours of the night.

## Day 80

Referring to his record-setting pace of enacting laws by Executive Order, the foreign press asks if he intends to rule by fiat. Trump responds, "Those pieces of shit? No way. It's Cadillac all the way for this president!"

## Day 81

"I'd like to think Americans deserves better," one world leader is quoted as saying, "But they did elect this jackass so, maybe not."

## Day 82

Asked if he plans to run for re-election, Trump replies, "I'll do whatever is necessary for the good of the country."

International newspaper headlines excitedly announce Trump's impending resignation.

## Day 83

A Wall Street Journal analysis of seven Trump-operated businesses concludes that, since he became U.S. president and stopped running them personally, four are no longer losing money, two have turned a small profit and one is projected to exceed estimated quarterly earnings by 15%.

## Day 84

The Walk-A-Back is now held every morning and renamed the "Oops-a-Daily."

## Day 85

Reports of sub-par materials, accounting irregularities, kickbacks and the widespread hiring of illegal immigrant labor on the construction of the Border Fence leads to an official investigation. President Trump accuses Mexico of starting the rumors, claiming, "They're just jealous they didn't get in on this deal when they had the chance."

## Day 86

Trump's tax filings for the previous two years show he has deducted the cost of everything (seriously, everything) he's done since the announcement of his candidacy and that the IRS now owes him $683 million.

## Day 87

Overseas factories of American companies are given full diplomatic status so that anything produced in them qualifies for the label "Made in the USA."

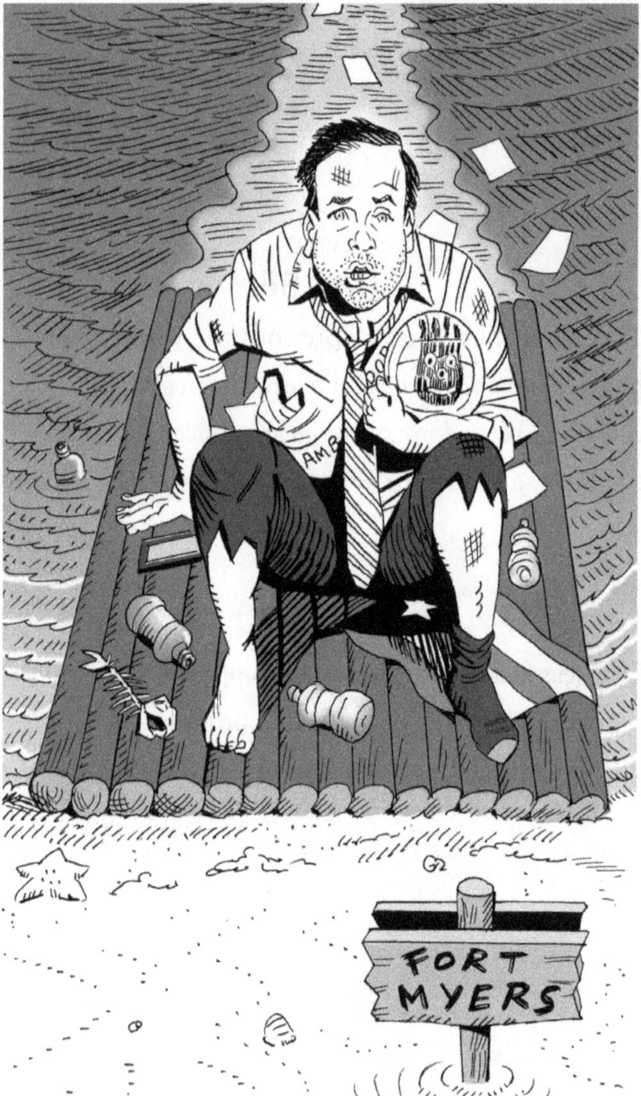
AMB
FORT MYERS

## Day 88

Sunburned and dehydrated, Marco Rubio washes up on Florida's Gulf Coast having escaped from Cuba on a raft.

## Day 89

Asked about his campaign promise to "Do something about my hair if elected," the president shrugs and replies, "I say a lot of things."

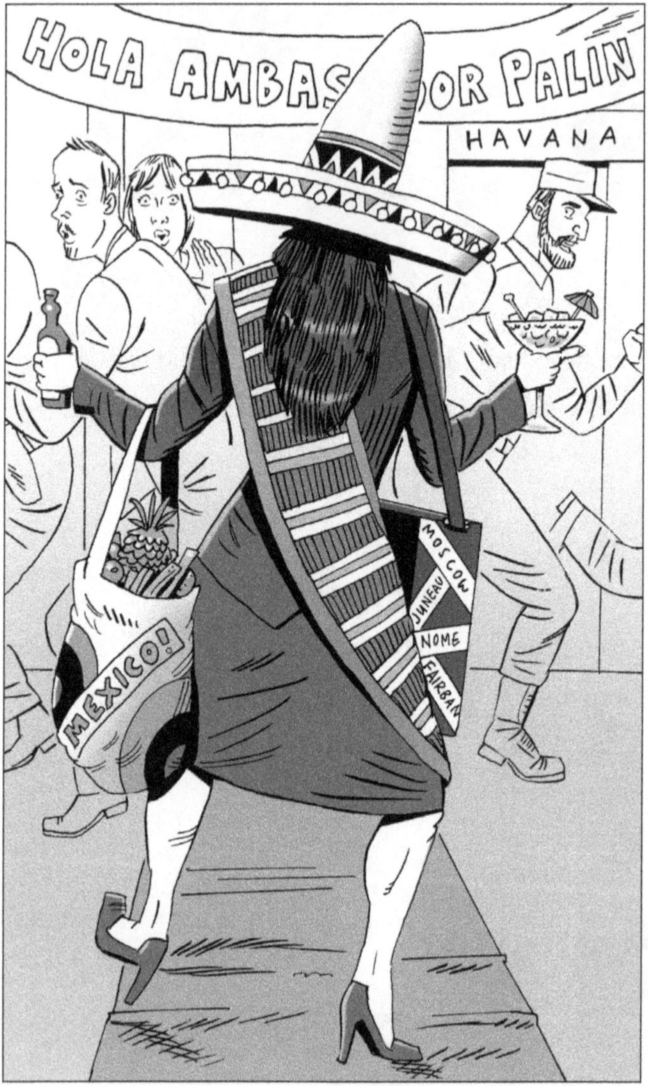
HOLA AMBAS DOR PALIN
HAVANA
MOSCOW
JUNEAU
NOME
FAIRBAN
MEXICO!

## Day 90

President Trump recalls Sarah Palin from Russia to take over the diplomatic mission in Cuba, saying, "Maybe a nice-looking broad will do the trick with those hotheads."

## Day 91

Thirteen hours after leaving Moscow, Ambassador Palin arrives in Havana. Speaking to reporters at the airport, she expresses her delight at being in Cuba and her eagerness to take in the local customs and culture such as celebrating Cinco de Mayo in its native land and maybe running with some bulls. The Cuban translator assigned to Palin, knowing what happened to his Russian counterparts, bolts from the scene.

## Day 92

The discovery of several tunnels underneath the Border Fence prompts its new nickname, "The Torntilla Curtain."

## Day 93

The administration's questionable fiscal practices create unease in the international financial community and the U.S. credit rating is lowered dramatically.

## Day 94

A sudden shortage of translators in Cuba has Ambassador Palin getting by on her high school Spanish; perplexed but accommodating locals have repeatedly told her how to get to the library and given her beer and nachos.

# Day 95

Trump incorporates the United States under the laws
of Delaware and announces an IPO of USA Inc.®,
decreeing that from this day forward the country will be
"For and of its citizen shareholders!" who are entitled
to gaming chips of equal value to the amount of their
dividends, redeemable at any Trump-owned casino
resort in the continental U.S.

# Day 96

President and CEO Trump moves all of USA Inc.®'s
available cash into an offshore account in the Cayman
Islands.

Congress hastily draws up articles of impeachment.

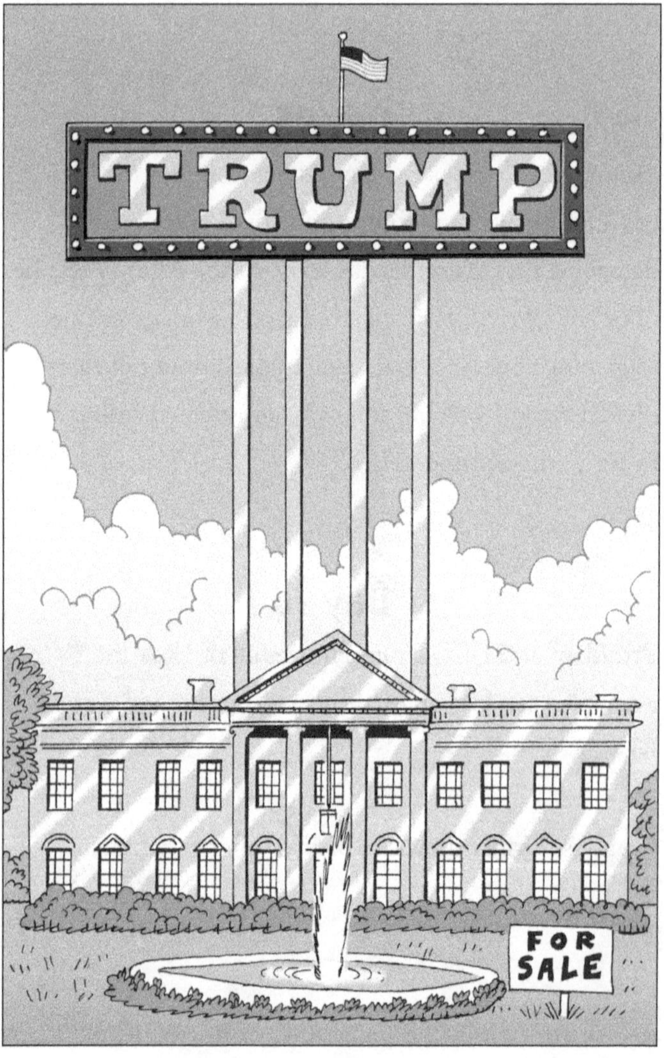
TRUMP
FOR SALE

## Day 97

China calls in the U.S.'s debt.

## Day 98

Trump declares USA Inc.® bankrupt and claims it is now under Chapter 11 protection.

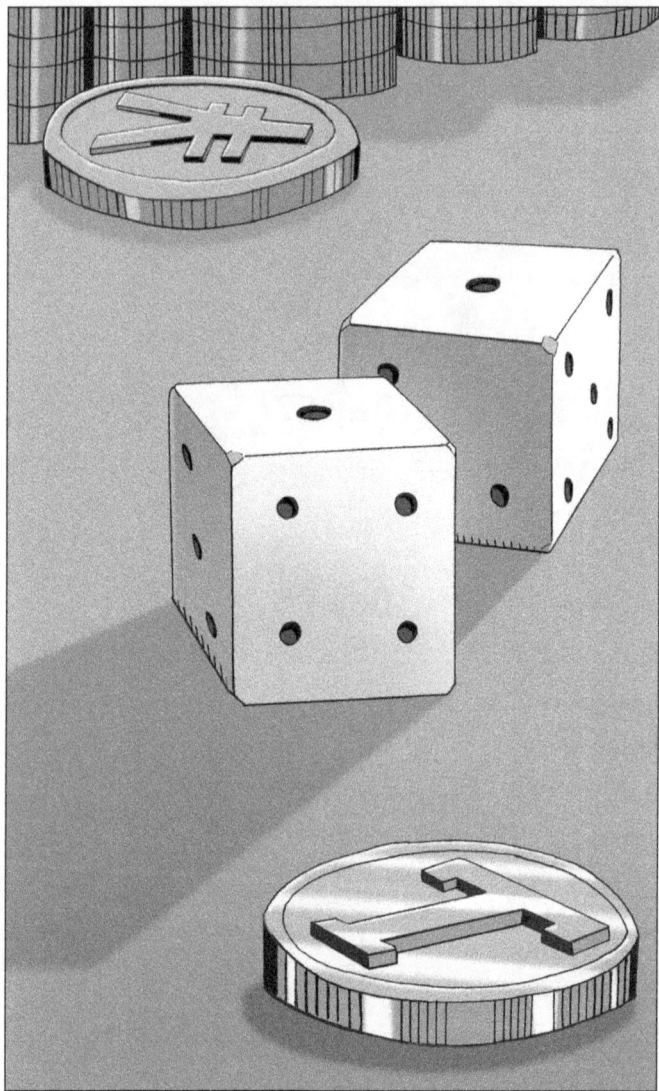

## Day 99

China declares war.

## Day 100

President Trump offers the Chinese government
gaming chips equal in value to the amount of the debt,
redeemable at any Trump-owned casino resort in the
continental U.S.

www.ingramcontent.com/pod-product-compliance
Lightning Source LLC
Chambersburg PA
CBHW031611040426
42452CB00006B/474
* 9 7 8 0 9 9 6 2 3 6 6 3 8 *